ANIMALS

Warthogs

by Kevin J. Holmes

Consultant:
Michele Rudovsky
Associate Curator
San Francisco Zoo

Bridgestone Books
an imprint of Capstone Press
Mankato, Minnesota

Bridgestone Books are published by Capstone Press
151 Good Counsel Drive, P.O. Box 669, Mankato, Minnesota, 56002
http://www.capstone-press.com

Library of Congress Cataloging-in-Publication Data
Holmes, Kevin J.
    Warthogs/by Kevin J. Holmes.
        p. cm.—(Animals)
    Includes bibliographical references and index.
    Summary: Introduces the warthog's physical characteristics, habits, food, and relationship
to humans.
    ISBN 0-7368-0067-0
    1. Warthog—Juvenile literature. [1. Warthog.] I. Title. II. Series: Animals (Mankato, Minn.)
QL737.U58H65 1999
599.63'3—dc21

                                                                                    98-17330
                                                                                         CIP
                                                                                          AC

Editorial Credits
Matt Doeden, editor; Timothy Halldin, cover designer; Sheri Gosewisch, photo researcher

Photo Credits
James P. Rowan, cover
Michele Burgess, 8
Tom & Pat Leeson, 14, 18
Visuals Unlimited/William J. Pohley, 4; Ken Lucas, 6; Mark Newman, 10; Gil Lopez-Espina, 12;
    Will Troyer, 16; Walt Anderson, 20

Table of Contents

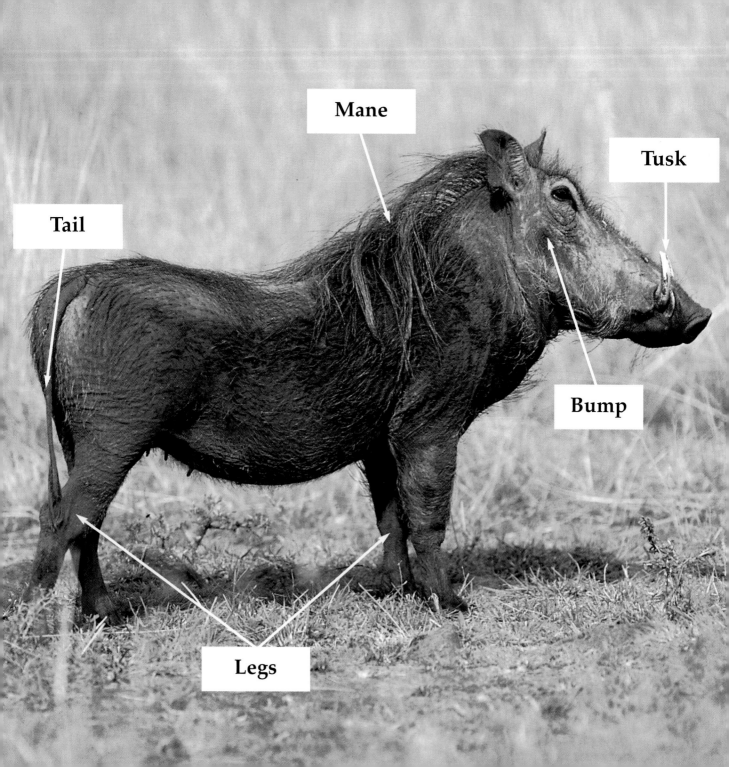

Fast Facts

Family: Warthogs belong to the *Suidae* family. A family is a group of animals with similar features. Pigs are also in the *Suidae* family.

Range: Warthogs live in central Africa.

Habitat: Warthogs live on savannas and in lightly forested areas. A savanna is flat, grassy land with few trees.

Food: Warthogs eat mostly grasses and other plants that grow on savannas.

Mating: Male warthogs sometimes fight for females during mating season. Mating season is during May and June.

Young: Young warthogs are called piglets.

Warthogs

Warthogs belong to the *Suidae* family. A family is a group of animals with similar features. Pigs are also in the *Suidae* family.

Warthogs are mammals. Mammals are warm-blooded animals with backbones. The body heat of warm-blooded animals stays about the same. Their body heat does not change with the weather.

Warthogs live mainly on the savannas of central Africa. A savanna is flat, grassy land with few trees. Warthogs eat grasses and other plants that grow on savannas.

Most warthogs have bumps on their faces that look like warts. That is why people named these animals warthogs.

Most warthogs have bumps on their faces.

Appearance

Warthogs are easy to recognize. They look something like pigs. Warthogs have gray skin, thin legs, and long tails. Most adult warthogs weigh between 130 and 250 pounds (59 and 113 kilograms). Their bodies are about four feet (1.2 meters) long. Males are larger than females.

Warthogs have manes of hair around their faces and necks. Male warthogs have thicker manes than females have.

Warthogs have bumps on their faces. These bumps are bigger on males than on females. Male warthogs sometimes fight. The bumps protect their faces during fights.

Warthogs have tusks. These long, pointed teeth stick out of their mouths. Most warthogs' tusks are about 12 inches (30 centimeters) long.

Warthogs have long, pointed tusks.

Homes

Warthogs live in central Africa. Most live on savannas. Some warthogs live in lightly forested areas. Warthogs eat grasses that grow in these locations.

Warthogs live near water because they need it to stay cool. Warthogs do not sweat like most mammals. Their bodies cannot cool themselves. Warthogs roll in mud to stay cool. They may die if they become too hot.

Warthogs live in dens, but they rarely dig dens for themselves. They usually live in dens made by aardvarks and other animals.

Warthogs' dens have small entrances. These small entrances protect warthogs from their enemies. Warthogs can fit through the entrances easily. But many other animals cannot fit through the small entrances.

Warthogs need water to stay cool.

Mating

Warthogs mate only during mating season. This is when they join together to produce young. Mating season is during May and June. Adult male warthogs live near females during mating season. They live alone for the rest of the year.

Two male warthogs may fight for a female. They push each other with their faces and tusks. The male who pushes the other warthog back wins the fight.

The male that wins the fight approaches the female. The male tries to begin mating. The female decides whether to mate with the male. Males do not stay with females after mating.

Female warthogs give birth about 170 days after mating. They usually give birth to three or four young.

Two male warthogs may fight for a female.

Young

Young warthogs are called piglets. Piglets look like adult warthogs, but the bumps on their faces are smaller. Their manes are shorter too.

Piglets are born in dens. They stay in the dens for about one week. They drink milk from their mothers' bodies. Piglets do not leave the dens without their mothers.

Piglets begin grazing two or three weeks after birth. They graze on grasses and other plants. Piglets line up neatly behind their mothers when they graze.

Warthog families are called sounders. Sounders may have up to three adult females and their young. Females may stay in the same sounders all their lives. Young male warthogs stay in their sounders for two years. Adult males live on their own.

Warthog families are called sounders.

Food

Warthogs eat mostly grasses and other plants. They eat roots, bulbs, and tubers. Tubers are thick, underground stems of some plants. Warthogs also eat tree bark, fallen fruit, and carrion. Carrion is flesh from dead animals.

Warthogs use their strong sense of smell to find food. First, they sniff the ground. Then they use their tusks to dig up the food. They must bend on their front knees to dig. Warthogs have thick skin on their knees. The skin protects their knees while they dig.

Warthogs are in danger when they bend on their knees. Predators can approach warthogs that are in this position. Predators hunt and eat other animals.

Warthogs must bend on their front knees to dig for food.

Enemies

Lions, leopards, and hyenas are predators that hunt warthogs. Warthogs have several ways of guarding themselves against these predators.

Warthogs have a sharp sense of smell and good hearing. They can usually smell or hear approaching predators. Warthogs have poor vision. But their eyes are high on their heads. This allows them to watch for predators while they eat.

Warthogs usually run away when predators come too near. Warthogs can run more than 30 miles (48 kilometers) per hour. They can run this fast only for short periods.

Warthogs run to their dens if they can. They enter their dens tail-first. That way, they can protect the dens with their tusks. They may fight predators that try to enter their dens.

Warthogs protect their dens with their tusks.

Warthogs and People

Warthogs usually avoid people. They stay away from large cities. But warthogs will protect themselves when they meet people. Warthogs that sense danger may attack people. Warthog mothers with piglets are most likely to attack people.

Some people hunt warthogs. Hunters kill them for their tusks and for meat. Hunters have forced warthogs out of some areas. In the past, warthogs were common in southern Africa. Today, few are left in that area.

Some African countries have passed laws against killing warthogs. These laws protect food supplies for animals such as lions. The laws keep warthog populations high.

Warthogs usually avoid people.

Hands on: Smelling Test

Warthogs rely on their sense of smell to live. You can test your sense of smell with this game.

What You Need

Eight people
Eight cotton balls
Eight glasses
Four liquids with strong scents. You can use vanilla, peppermint, lemon, and vinegar.

What You Do

1. Soak two cotton balls in each liquid.
2. Place one cotton ball in each of the glasses.
3. Ask each person to take a glass. Do not tell people which scents they have.
4. Ask each person to find the person who has the same scent. The people should stand together when they find one another.
5. Put the glasses down and try again. You may want to add new scents.

Words to Know

carrion (KAR-ee-uhn)—flesh from dead animals
graze (GRAYZ)—to eat grass and other plants
mammal (MAM-uhl)—a warm-blooded animal with a backbone
mane (MAYN)—hair around an animal's face and neck
predator (PRED-uh-tur)—an animal that hunts and eats other animals
savanna (suh-VAN-uh)—flat, grassy land with few trees
tuber (TOO-bur)—the thick, underground stem of a plant
tusk (TUHSK)—a long, pointed tooth

Read More

Rothaus, Don P. *Warthogs.* Nature Books. Plymouth, Minn.: The Child's World, 1996.

Silver, Donald M. *African Savanna.* One Small Square. New York: Learning Triangle Press, 1997.

Useful Addresses

Fort Worth Zoo
1989 Colonial Parkway
Fort Worth, TX 76110

Toronto Zoo
361A Old Finch Avenue
Scarborough, Ontario M1B 5K7
Canada

Internet Sites

San Francisco Zoo/Warthog
http://www.sfzoo.com/html/map.warthog.html

Warthog
www.scz.org/animals/w/warthog.html

Index